6

Which of these inventions would you like to see firs~~t~~

D1064077

Circle one.

3) A work-out in a pill
4) Flying cars
5) Everlasting lip balm

9

Which of these predictions have the best chance of coming true?

Rank these options from 1 to 5.

Ten years from now...

A. ... I will have run a marathon.
B. ... I will own a dog.
C. ... I will have appeared on TV.
D. ... I'll still have the same best friend.
E. ... my closet will be tidy and organized.

In 40 years, would you rather...?

Pick one.

a. Feel old and cranky, but look fantastic
b. Feel fantastic but look like an old crank

8

What fortune would you like to find in your next fortune cookie?

Fill in your answer.

7

10

What are you looking forward to the most about your life 20 years from now?

Fill in the blank.

LOVE & Crushes & Stuff

Grab a response sheet to fill in your answers.

1.
Have you ever been in love before?
Circle your answer.
A. Totally. In fact, I'm in love right now.
B. Yes, I was, but not anymore.
C. No, but I'd like to be.
D. I'm not sure. Love is confusing.
E. Eww! No!

You're Cute

2.
How in love are you right now?
Circle where you land on the scale.

1 — Madly in love
2 — A little lovey-dovey
3 — Fondly friendly
4 — Mildly in like
5 — Currently love-free

3.
Love at first sight is totally real.
Circle your response.

5.
Make a pie chart of your heart. Who or what is cherished there?
Put your answer in the circle.

Mike

ice cream

my family

volley-ball

4.
Be honest!
Fill in your answers.
a) Out of everyone you know, who makes (or would make) the cutest couple?

b) Who would be a TERRIBLE couple?

c) Who has been in love the most times?

d) Who is a great big flirt?

e) Who makes your heart go pitter-pat?

to:

6.

Which names would you like your sweetie to call you?

Circle at least two.

1) Snookums
2) Sugar Pie
3) Honey
4) Pumpkin
5) Dude

7.

Describe your dream date.

Fill in your answer.

Be Mine

8.

Who would you rather date?

Pick one.

a. An Olympic-medal-winning athlete

b. A Grammy-winning singer

9.

What do you enjoy about crushing on someone?

Rank these options from 1 to 5.

A. That feeling of nervous excitement

B. Daydreaming non-stop (like, obsessing) about someone

C. Planning what you are going to wear or do or say next time you see each other

D. Wondering how the object of your affection feels about you

E. Getting teased about it by your friends

10.

If I had to describe my love life in one word, it would be...

Fill in the blank.

VACATIONS & TRAVEL

Grab a response sheet to fill in your answers.

1 We're going to pack our bags and leave tonight. Where to?

Circle your answer.

A. Snorkeling at a coral reef in Australia

B. Getting fitted for fancy fashions in Paris

C. Tracking wild animals on a photo safari in Africa

D. Experiencing zero gravity in outer space

E. Anywhere there is hot sun, a warm pool, and an icy drink

2 Can you travel light?

Circle where you land on the scale.

1 Just let me grab my toothbrush and we're gone.

2 The toothbrush and a backpack is all I need.

3 My toothbrush, one backpack, and a little travel bag with wheels.

4 Toothbrush, backpack, little wheelie thing, plus a big old suitcase.

5 I need all that stuff, plus another suitcase for everything I'm going to buy when we get there.

5 This circle is your window at your dream vacation destination. Draw the view.

Put your answer in the circle.

4 Be honest!

Fill in your answers.

a) What's the most exotic or distant destination you have ever visited?

b) If you won a weekend in Hawaii or a week in Dallas, which would you pick?

c) If you could take five people with you on that trip you won, who would you bring?

d) Put down five words that describe a typical road trip in a car with your family.

e) What's the best thrill ride you've ever been on?

3 When you toast marshmallows over a fire, do you burn them on purpose?

Circle your response.

FLUFFY PUFF

18

6 If you absolutely had to, which things could you give up completely for one whole summer vacation?
Circle at least two.

1) TV
2) Phone
3) Computer
4) Tunes
5) Texting

FOOD

AIRPORT

8 Which would you rather have tomorrow?
Pick one.
a. A boring vacation day
b. An interesting school day

7 Say you are running your own sleep-away summer camp. What is it called, and what do campers do there?
Fill in your answer.

CAMP

9 What's the most awesome part about a day at the beach or pool?
Rank these options from 1 to 5.
A. Being seen in a bathing suit
B. Swimming
C. Lying in the sun
D. Cooling off near the water
E. Splashing and goofing around

10 Which is better – summer vacation or winter holidays? Why?
Fill in the blank.

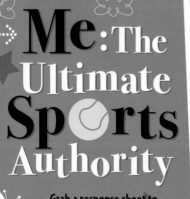

Me: The Ultimate Sports Authority

Grab a response sheet to fill in your answers.

1

Which are your strongest athletic events?

Circle your answer.

A. Solo Challenges
   (like long-distance running)

B. Team Sports (like volleyball)

C. Extreme Sports
   (like white-water rafting)

D. Gymnastics (or dance,
   or cheerleading...)

E. Reclining (involving a
   hammock, maybe, and a book)

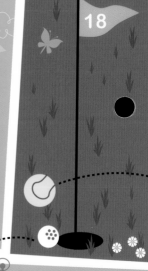

2

Are you a big sports fan?

Circle where you land on the scale.

1 Uh, no

2 I'll watch if there's nothing else on

3 Sports can be fun

4 Yeah, I'm a big fan

5 We're #1! We're #1!
   Wait, what was the question?

3

Snowboarding is way cooler than skiing.

Circle your response.

4

Be honest!

Fill in your answers.

a) What is your favorite sports team?

b) Which sports team do you hate the most?

c) Do you ever wear clothes featuring a team logo? What team?

d) In which Olympic event would you love to compete?

e) Do you think ballroom dancing is a sport? Why or why not?

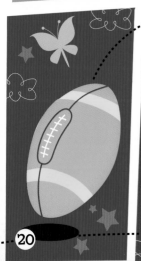

5

If you were starting a professional sports team, what would their team name logo look like?

Put your answer in the circle.

6

If you were absolutely required to go out for two sports teams at school, which would you choose?

Circle at least two.

1) Synchronized swimming
2) Sumo wrestling
3) Platform diving
4) Roller derby
5) Bull fighting

7

Is it more fun to watch sports or play sports. Why?

Fill in your answer.

8

Would you rather... ?

Pick one.

a. Be the best player on a losing team
b. Be the worst player on a winning team

9

What do you like the most about playing sports?

Rank these options from 1 to 5.

A. Getting all sweaty and healthy
B. The togetherness of being on a team
C. The thrill of competition
D. Wearing cool athletic gear
E. Having people watch you play

10

Which sports would you like to try someday?

Fill in the blank.

TRUE CONFESSIONS
When I Was Little...
Grab a response sheet to fill in your answers.

1 When you were little, did you believe any of these things?

Circle your answer(s).

A. Swallow a seed and it will sprout in your tummy.

B. Your toys come alive at night.

C. Step on a crack, break your mother's back.

D. Parents have eyes in the back of their heads.

E. Dig a deep enough hole and you'll end up on the other side of the world.

2 How would your last babysitter describe you?

Circle where you land on the scale.

1 An angel who was perfect in every way

2 A charming child who tried to do the right thing

3 A regular kid who sometimes messed up

4 A brat she had to watch at all times

5 A terror that still haunts her nightmares

3

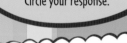

It was more fun to be little than it is to be my current age.

Circle your response.

4 Be honest! Fill in your answers.

When you were a kid...

a) Did you ever cut your own hair? Did you ever cut a doll's hair?

b) Did you sleep with your door open or shut? Was the light on or off?

c) Who was your favorite cartoon character?

d) What was the goofiest thing you thought was true?

e) Who did you think was the coolest person in the world?

5 Draw a picture of your family like you used to draw them when you were little.

Put your answer in the circle.

6

What do you miss most about being a little kid?

Circle one.

1) Finger painting
2) Having someone kiss your boo-boos
3) No school
4) Getting tucked in at night
5) Playing pretend

7

Describe a stuffed animal you used to sleep with. Do you still sleep with it?

Fill in your answer.

8

Which were you?

Pick one.

a. The noisy, wild-and-crazy, running-around-screaming kid
b. The quiet, shy, mousy, hiding-behind-Mom kid

9

If you had a playdate, which of these things would be the most fun?

Rank these options from 1 to 5.

A. Spinning around and around until you were fall-down dizzy
B. Playing with dolls like Barbie or Bratz
C. Tickle fights
D. Playing dress-up
E. Building pillow forts

10

What was the first thing you ever wanted to be when you grew up?

Fill in the blank.

SHERIFF

Just my Style
shopping and FASHION

Grab a response sheet to fill in your answers.

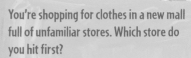

1

You're shopping for clothes in a new mall full of unfamiliar stores. Which store do you hit first?

Circle your answer.

A. Lilly Belle's Boutique of Frilly Frocks

B. House of Rivets: All Denim Everything

C. Retro-A-Go-Go: For That Vintage Vibe

D. Cozy MacFleece's Super Comfy Fuzzy Duds

E. Dazzle: A Gallery of Glittery Glam Gowns

2

Do you follow the latest fashion trends?

Circle where you land on the scale.

1 I hate trends.

2 Meh. I don't pay attention to trends.

3 I try to be trendy.

4 I'm totally trendy!

5 I'm the one that sets the trends, darling!

3

Clothes look better if they have a brand logo on them.

Circle your response.

4

Be honest!

Fill in your answers.

a) Which of the things you are wearing today do you love the most, and why?

b) Do you own any clothing that is tie-dyed?

c) Would you wear real fur? Why or why not?

d) What is the most recent item of clothing you borrowed from someone?

e) If you could copy any celebrity's fashion style, who would it be?

5

Draw a pie chart that shows where your current wardrobe came from.

Put your answer in the circle.

Hand-me-downs · Lacy's · Eternally 19 · Nickerbocker + Flitch · Thrift stores

6

If you absolutely had to pick from among these items, which would you wear to school?

Circle at least two.

1) A tutu
2) Shiny spandex pants
3) A hat with earflaps
4) Scuba flippers
5) A live snake

7

If you were starting your own fashion line, what kind of clothes would you design?

Fill in your answer.

8

Tube tops.

Pick one.

a. Tacky
b. Tasteful

9

What do you like the most about shopping?

Rank these options from 1 to 5.

A. Trying on cool outfits
B. Hanging out with friends at the mall
C. Free perfume samples
D. Seeing the latest fashions in the stores
E. Two words: food court

10

Describe your style in three words.

Fill in the blank.

BOOKS, MOVIES, TV & ME

Grab a response sheet to fill in your answers.

1 In your craziest dreams, which TV talent show would you most like to win?

Circle your answer.

A. A be-a-pop-star singing contest

B. A gourmet cooking competition

C. A national spelling bee

D. A contest to be a super model

E. A fashion design competition

2 When it comes to reading, how do you see yourself?

Circle where you land on the scale.

1 Total, utter, and complete bookworm.

2 It's fun to curl up with a good book every once in a while.

3 I'm more of a magazine queen, myself.

4 I read. But mostly for school and stuff.

5 I'd really rather be online or chatting with friends.

3 Will you share your tub o' popcorn at the movies?

Circle your response.

4 Be honest!

Fill in your answers.

a) If someone wrote a tell-all book about you, what would it be called?

b) If you could only watch one TV channel for an entire year, which would you pick?

c) What's the last book you read just for fun?

d) Would you rather direct a movie, write the screenplay, or be the star?

e) What was your favorite holiday TV special when you were a kid?

5 Jot down your favorite movie, TV, or book quote.

Put your answer in the circle.

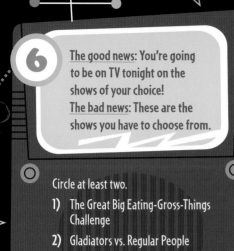

6

The good news: You're going to be on TV tonight on the shows of your choice!
The bad news: These are the shows you have to choose from.

Circle at least two.

1) The Great Big Eating-Gross-Things Challenge
2) Gladiators vs. Regular People
3) The Humiliating Home Videos Hour
4) Ambush: The Head-to-Toe Makeover Show
5) The 11 O'Clock News

7

In the movie version of your life, who would play you and your friends?

Fill in your answer.

8

Chatting mid-movie.
Pick one.
a. That's fine.
b. Total crime!

9

S.O.S

If you were stuck on a deserted island, which would you most like to have as company?

Rank these options from 1 to 5.

A. An infinite supply of paper and pens so you could document your time on the island

B. An itty-bitty TV, hooked up to every channel in the world

C. An entire library stocked with thousands of wonderful books

D. A ginormous movie screen and 50 of your all-time fave flicks

E. One ratty copy of **Cat Fancy** magazine from the year you were born, and your best friend.

10

If you were a famous cartoon character, who would you be?

Fill in the blank.

the TRUTH aBOUT LYInG, SeCReTS & GOSSiP

1. Grab a response sheet to fill in your answers.

Whose secrets would you most love to know? Circle your answer.

A. The mysterious 'rents

D. A sibling

B. Your most intriguing teacher

E. The President of the United States

C. The most popular kid at school

2. 'Fess up: How honest are you, really? Circle where you land on the scale.

1 I pretty much tell it exactly like it is. No white lies, no sugarcoating.

2 I'll tell a little fib here and there, but nothing major.

3 Depends on the case. Depends on the consequences.

4 I only lie when it's really, really, really convenient. So... pretty often.

5 I've never – not even once ever – told a lie. Swear.
   (OK, truth is, I do it quite a lot.)

3. People are way too obsessed with gossiping about the rich and famous.

Circle your response.

4. Be honest! Fill in your answers.

a) What's the stupidest rumor you've ever heard?

b) What would you write in a diary that you wouldn't post on a blog?

c) If you could start a rumor about yourself, what would it be?

d) If there were a mood ring that really told people exactly what you were feeling, would you wear it? Always? Never? When?

e) What do you think people lie about the most?

5. Call this your trust circle. Put the people you know you can confide in here. Jot down their names or draw their faces – or both!

Put your answer in the circle.

6.

You accidentally found out that Miss Popular is going to be "kidnapped" on her birthday morning and brought to school in her jammies. What do you do?

Circle one.

1) Tell her quick so she has time to buy cute p.j.s!
2) Keep it to yourself
3) Tell everyone in school so they don't miss the show
4) Drop mysterious hints so she knows something's up, but no details
5) Bring a camera to class

7.

Your best friend asks what you think of her new (bad!) haircut. What do you say?

Fill in your answer.

8.

Which do you choose?

Pick one.

a. Truth   b. Dare

9.

Which of these resolutions would be hardest to keep for a solid year?

Rank these options from 1 to 5.

A. No lying of any kind, white or otherwise
B. You can't question anything anyone says to you
C. All your secrets must be made public
D. Whenever anyone asks "How are you?" you have to answer in great and truthful detail
E. No gossip for you, no matter how juicy

10.

At your school, what's the hot topic for gossip?

Fill in the blank.

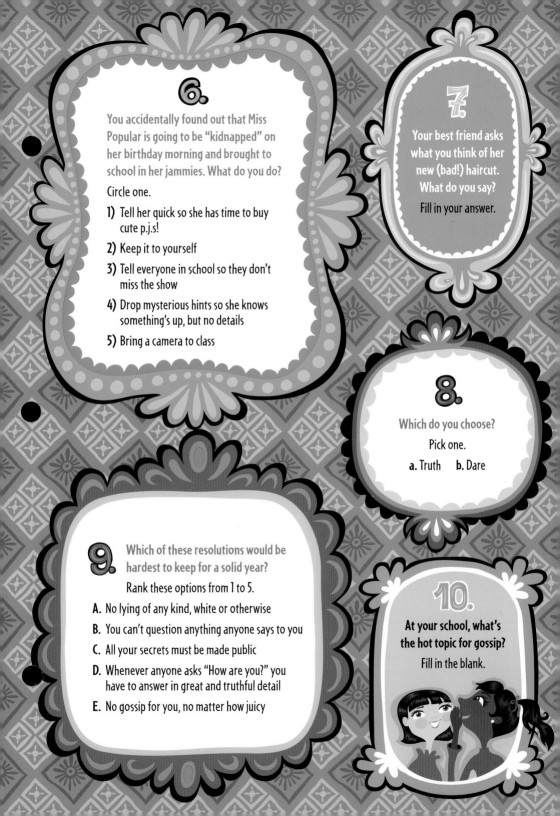

The Truth About CATS & DOGS & Other Critters

Grab a response sheet to fill in your answers.

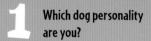

1 Which dog personality are you?

Circle your answer.

A. A fierce and loyal Doberman pinscher

B. An observant and intelligent dachshund

C. A ridiculously friendly Labrador retriever

D. A snuggly widdle pug princess

E. Like I would ever be a dog. As if.

2 How animal-crazy are you?

Circle where you land on the scale.

1 I may be crazy, but not for animals. Pass.

2 I like animals, but I like people a lot more.

3 Life is better with a dog. Or a cat.

4 Or a wombat. Any animal, really. I love them all!

5 All my best friends have four legs.

3

Dressing up your dog is a fabulous thing to do.

Circle your response.

4 Be honest!

Fill in your answers.

a) Have you ever bought a gift for an animal? What was it?

b) Are you a cat person or a dog person? Or a something-else person?

c) Are circuses better with animals or without them?

d) Do you bite the heads off animal crackers?

e) Were you scared of any animals when you were a kid? Which one(s)?

5

If your pet (or another animal you know) could talk, what would it say?

Put your answer in the circle.

6

If your parents said you absolutely had to keep some of your brother's pets in your bedroom, which would you pick?

Circle at least two.

1) Skunk
2) Tarantula
3) Potbellied pig
4) Madagascar hissing cockroach
5) Piranha

7

Describe the most wonderful pet you've ever known.

Fill in your answer.

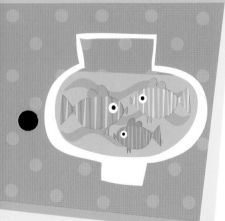

8

Which would you rather have?

Pick one.

a. Wings.
b. A tail. And super-great hearing. And retractable claws.

9

Which of these animals would be your dream pet?

Rank these options from 1 to 5.

A. Horse
B. Poodle
C. Tiger cub
D. Python
E. Canary

10

If you could be any breed of animal for a day, which would you be and why?

Fill in the blank.

MY SCHOOL
Confidential

Grab a response sheet to
fill in your answers.

1 If you had to do a huge final project
to graduate, which would you pick?
Circle your answer.

A. Perform a solo evening of
Shakespeare for the entire school

B. Solve a super complex math
problem – show your work!

C. Research and write a history of
your school, with photos, footnotes,
and interviews

D. Do a chemical analysis of the
cafeteria's mystery meat

E. Write a piece of original music
and conduct the marching band
in performing it

2 How stressed do you get
about tests?

Circle where you land on the scale.

1 Tests totally freak me out.

2 I get nervous before every
test I take.

3 Sometimes I'm ready to
kick test butt. But not always.
Way not always.

4 If I studied, I'm good. And I
study all the time.

5 Usually tests are a cool breeze
for me. Sometimes they're
even fun.

3
I get a little buzz of happy
excitement at the start of
each new school year.
Circle your response.

4 Be honest!
Fill in your answers.

At your school, who is most likely to...

a) Make you laugh?

b) Be elected president someday?

c) Star in their own reality series?

d) Start a bazillion-dollar company?

e) Hitchhike around the world?

5
If you could make your school
mascot anything you want,
what would it be? Draw or
describe it here, please.

Put your answer in the circle.

6 After you graduate, what will you miss most about your days at this school?
Circle at least two.

1) The brilliant teachers
2) Your charming classmates
3) The scrumptious cafeteria food
4) The fascinating homework
5) The thrilling dances and other social events

7 Describe your dream field trip.
Fill in your answer.

8 Which type of school would you rather attend?
Pick one.
a. Single-sex   b. Co-ed

9 Which of these things would you most like to be?
Rank these options from 1 to 5.
A. Homecoming queen
B. Star of the student musical
C. Valedictorian
D. Athlete of the year
E. Teacher's pet

10 If you had the power to add any class to the curriculum at your school, what would it be?
Fill in the blank.

the SCOOP on FOOD

Grab a response sheet to fill in your answers.

1

Which sounds like the most perfect meal for you?

Circle your answer.

A. Lobster at an elegant restaurant

B. Cotton candy and a burger at an amusement park

C. A big salad at a sidewalk cafe

D. Hot dogs cooked over a fire on the beach

E. Waffles and orange juice in bed

2

When you do the cooking, is the food any good?

Circle where you land on the scale.

1 Mouth-wateringly fabulous

2 Yummy!

3 Totally edible

4 Well, it's food

5 Ick. I'll call for a pizza.

3

Hot sauce totally rocks!

Circle your response.

4

Be honest!

Fill in your answers.

a) What was the last thing you ate?

b) Who is the best cook you know?

c) What is your favorite restaurant?

d) What's the nastiest thing you ever ate?

e) What's your favorite junk food?

5

Draw the tastiest meal ever on this plate. Label each delicious thing.

Put your answer in the circle.

6

If you had to order lunch off this menu, what would you pick?

Circle at least two.

1) Tongue
2) Liver and onions
3) Eel
4) Octopus
5) Anchovy pizza with extra anchovies

7

Describe your dream wedding cake.

Fill in your answer.

Red or black

8

You can have only one kind of licorice for the rest of your life.

Pick one.

a. Black   **b.** Red

9

Which dessert do you prefer? Rank these options from 1 to 5.

A. Strawberry ice cream
B. Butterscotch pudding
C. Peanut butter cookies
D. Apple pie
E. Whatever it is, it's chocolate

cookie

ice cream

JeLL-O

Pudding

whip cream

fruit

10

Right now I am hungry for...

Fill in the blank.

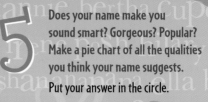

my real names

Grab a response sheet to fill in your answers.

1 Do you like the name you got when you were born? Circle your answer.

A. I love it! It is, without doubt, the most fabulous name in the universe.

B. Yes, I like it. It fits me.

C. Eh. It's all right, I guess.

D. Hate it. What were they thinking?

E. What name? That name is so not me, I don't even acknowledge it.

2 How cool is your middle name?

Circle where you land on the scale.

1 Ultra super mega cool

2 I like it fine

3 Whatever

4 A bit embarassing, actually

5 Hideously dorky

3 If a girl's name ends in -y or -ie, she seems cuter.

Circle your response.

5 Does your name make you sound smart? Gorgeous? Popular? Make a pie chart of all the qualities you think your name suggests. Put your answer in the circle.

friendly
cute
short
Irish

4 Be honest!

Fill in your answers.

a) If you could give yourself any name in the world, what would it be?

b) What did you name your first pet or stuffed animal?

c) If you had been born the other gender, what would you have been named?

d) What nicknames have you had?

e) What name or nickname do you hate to be called the most?

6 If you had to name your children after these actual celebrity babies, which would you pick?

Circle at least two.

1) Pilot Inspektor
2) Moxie CrimeFighter
3) Duncan Zowie Heywood
4) Audio Science
5) Daisy Boo

7 Say you're creating a new super heroine. What would you name her and why?

Fill in your answer.

8 What would you rather be named?
Pick one.
a. Ima Hogg
b. Anita Bath

9 How do you like these names?
Rank these options from 1 to 5.
A. Dot   D. Madison
B. Shakeela   E. Zerlinda
C. Ethel

10 If I could give myself any name in the world, it would be...
Fill in the blank.

TRULY EMBARRASSING MOMENTS

Grab a response sheet to fill in your answers.

1 Have you ever done any of the following? Circle your answer(s).

A. Loudly and unexpectedly burped in front of people

B. Walked into a plate-glass door or wall

C. Accidently dropped a tray in a cafeteria

D. Walked around with your pants unzipped

E. Smiled in the mirror and found something disgusting between your teeth

BURP

2 How embarrassing are your parents?

Circle where you land on the scale.

1 Honestly, I think I embarrass **them**.

2 They're pretty cool, actually.

3 Occasionally embarrassing.

4 They'd be okay if they just didn't talk.

5 Embarrassing isn't the word. Try "horrifying."

3 Seeing other people get humiliated is hilarious.

Circle your response.

4 Be honest!

Fill in your answers.

a) Describe your most embarrassing baby picture.

b) What is the most embarrassing thing you've ever done in a dream?

c) Have you ever sung a karaoke song? What song did you sing?

d) Do you currently own any undies with cartoon characters on them? Describe them.

e) Who would be the worst person to see you make a fool of yourself?

5 Draw your expression when you get really, truly, totally embarrassed.

Put your answer in the circle.

6 Okay, it's not going to be the prom of your dreams. Which humiliation would be the most hideous?

Circle one.

1) Your date is your brother.
2) You and this other girl are wearing the exact same dress.
3) Your parents are chaperoning. And they're dancing.
4) Your date tells you there's spinach in your teeth. AFTER the photo.
5) You come out of the bathroom with your skirt tucked up. Way up.

7 Describe the most embarrassing thing you've ever experienced.

Fill in your answer.

8 Would you rather... ?

Pick one.

a. Walk into your own surprise party wearing nothing but a towel
b. Accidently announce the name of your crush over the school P.A. system

9 Which of these situations would embarrass you the most?

Rank these options from 1 to 5.

A. Ripping the seat of your pants
B. Falling down the stairs at school
C. Spilling a drink on yourself
D. Spilling a drink on your crush
E. Waving back at a cutie... who was not actually waving at you

10 Have you ever experienced an embarrassing bathing suit malfunction? Do tell.

Fill in the blank.

Me & My
One-of-a-Kind Family

Grab a response sheet to fill in your answers.

1. Which fictional family is most like your real family? Circle your answer.

A. The Incredibles

D. The Brady Bunch

B. The Berenstain Bears

E. The Simpsons

C. The Addams Family

2. Every family has its own particular brand of humor. What's yours like? Circle where you land on the scale.

1 We laugh all the time, at everything. We're kind of goofy that way.

2 In our family, if you're not being teased, you're not being loved.

3 We're funny, but we don't poke fun at each other. That's mean.

4 We're mostly pretty serious, but sometimes we have a good laugh.

5 Humor? Explain this word "humor," please.

3. If you could switch families with royalty – and become a real live princess – would you do it? Circle your response.

4. Be honest! Fill in your answers.

a) What do your parents nag you about the most?

b) If you could change your family's last name, what would you change it to?

c) Who do you consider your closest frelative? (friend + relative = frelative)

d) If Hollywood made a movie about your family, what should they call it?

e) Who in your family are you most like?

5. Your clan is having a huge family reunion and you've been volunteered to dream up the T-shirt. What will it look like?

Put your answer in the circle.

6. Your friends would probably say your house has the best... what?

Circle at least two.

1) Food and drinks
2) Toys and gizmos
3) Pets
4) Conversation and laughs
5) Mess

7. Copy this poem, adding your own words. Extra points for rhyming!

Roses are red. Diamonds are rare. My family rocks 'cause we have curly hair!

Fill in your answer.
Roses are red.
_____ are _____.
My family rocks
'Cause _____.

8. Surprise – you have a long-lost twin! You were separated at birth, but now she's coming to live with you.

Pick one.

a. That's great!
b. That stinks!

9. If you could pick your own family, which sibling situation would you like most?

Rank these options from 1 to 5.

A. One sister
B. One brother
C. One brother and one sister
D. More than two siblings
E. No sibs, please. Thanks anyway!

10.

In your family, who is most likely to be leading a secret life as an international spy?
Fill in the blank.

YIKES!
FEARS & SPOOKY STUFF

Grab a response sheet to fill in your answers.

1.

You get one roller coaster ride today. Which do you pick?

Circle your answer.

A. Beep-Beep Trolley Kiddie Coaster

B. The Zippity Zipper

C. Twister's Revenge

D. The Mighty Mega-Hurler

E. X-celerated Evil: The X-ecutioner

2.

How superstitious are you?

Circle where you land on the scale.

1 Not at all. I'd totally walk under a ladder just for the fun of it.

2 A tiny bit, but I'd walk under a ladder if it was in my way.

3 Sort of. I'd squeeze past a ladder to avoid going under it.

4 Very. I'd cross the street to avoid walking under a ladder.

5 Super-duper-stitious. Don't even talk to me about ladders.

3.

I like taking walks in graveyards.
Circle your response.

I.M. DEAD

4.

Be honest!

Fill in your answers.

a) What's the scariest movie you've ever seen?

b) When you were a kid, where were the monsters: under the bed or in the closet or...?

c) How much would you have to be paid to stay alone overnight in a strange, creepy house?

d) Would you get married on Friday the 13th?

e) Is there anything you used to be afraid of that doesn't scare you anymore?

5.

Draw your best portrait of Frankenstein's monster. Don't skimp on the bolts.

Put your answer in the circle.

42

6. If you had to meet two of these creatures in real life, which would you pick?

Circle at least two.

1) Vampire
2) Werewolf
3) Demon
4) Witch
5) Slimy green space alien

7. Do you believe in ghosts? Why or why not?

Fill in your answer.

8. Clowns. Pick one.

a. Terrific
b. Terrifying

9. How scary are these things? Rank these options from 1 to 5.

A. Snakes
B. Spiders
C. Getting a shot at the doctor's office
D. Making a speech in front of a crowd
E. Brain-eating zombies

10. If you were making a horror movie, what would you call it?

Fill in the blank.

IT'S MY PARTY!
CELEBRATIONS & GOOD TIMES

Grab a response sheet to fill in your answers.

1. What kind of party sounds like the most fun?

Circle your answer.

A. Hawaiian luau pool party

B. Girls-night-in spa slumber party

C. Surprise birthday party – and you're the surprised one!

D. All-night grad party at an amusement park

E. Co-ed costume dance party in the school gym

2. How much do you like to let loose and get your party on?

Circle where you land on the scale.

1 Parties are fine, but I'd rather curl up with a good book or movie.

2 I like small get-togethers with close friends. Big parties, not so much.

3 I tend to put in an appearance, enjoy myself, and head home on the early side.

4 I can get crazy sometimes. Not always, just sometimes.

5 Look up "party animal" in the dictionary. That's my picture there.

3. Do you plan your blow-out-the-candles birthday wish in advance?

Circle your response.

4. Be honest!

Fill in your answers.

a) How do you usually react when a group dance starts (like the Chicken Dance or the YMCA dance)?

b) The saying goes "It's better to give than to receive." Really?

c) What was the last party you went to?

d) What's the lamest party game?

e) If you could get any musical act in the world to perform at your next party, who would you get?

5. Design your dream party outfit.

Put your answer in the circle.

Your parents are helping you throw a party and they each want to be totally in charge of something, with no input from you. What will you let them pick?

Circle at least two.

1) The guest list – who you're inviting
2) The tunes
3) The food
4) The setting and decorations
5) Your clothes and hairstyle

How did you celebrate your last birthday?

Fill in your answer.

Which would you rather have at your party?

Pick one.

a. A super-deluxe make-your-own-hot-fudge-sundae ice-cream buffet
b. Boys

Which gift would you most like to get: a real-live pony, a cell phone, or world peace?

Fill in the blank.

Which days inspire the best parties?

Rank these options from 1 to 5.

A. Halloween
B. The first day of summer
C. Valentine's Day
D. Winter holidays
E. Hello? My birthday, obvs.

The Survey of Utter Randomosity

Grab a response sheet to fill in your answers.

1 Can you do any of the following?

Circle your answer(s).

A. Roll your tongue

B. Wiggle your ears

C. Lift only one eyebrow

D. Touch your nose with your tongue

E. Burp on demand

2

Which of these actual song titles best expresses your mood today?

Circle where you land on the scale.

1 "I'm So Excited"

2 "I Feel Good"

3 "Crazy"

4 "Dazed and Confused"

5 "Poor, Poor Pitiful Me"

3 Would you ever borrow someone else's toothbrush?

Circle your response.

4 Be honest! Fill in your answers.

a) What is your favorite school subject, besides lunch?

b) Who is the last person you spoke with on the phone? What about?

c) Ever broken any bones? Which, where, how?

d) Describe your dream car (or other vehicle).

e) What's your most annoying habit?

5 What doodle do you do most often?

Put your answer in the circle.

SWIMMING POOL CAR

6

A genie will give you two amazing skills. Which do you pick?

Circle just two.

1) You can do any math problem instantly in your head.

2) You can read minds.

3) You are the most physically coordinated person on Earth.

4) You know exactly the right thing to say in every situation.

5) Every day, perfect hair.

7

Who is the most famous person you've ever met or almost met? How do you know them (or kind of know them)? Details, please.

Fill in your answer.

8

Pick one.

a. Smooth

b. Chunky

9

Which of these dares would you be most likely to do for a million dollars?

Rank these options from 1 to 5.

A. Eat a bowl of cat food

B. Shave your head

C. Say nothing but "I am woman, hear me roar" for an entire day

D. Drink a jar of pickle juice

E. Wash your hair with toothpaste

10

Be honest! What do you like best about yourself?

Fill in the blank.

When you want to re-read someone's finished survey...

1.

POP OPEN
the binder rings.

2.

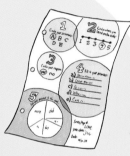

TAKE OUT their response form and shut the rings again.

3.

FLIP TO THE PAGE
number written on the response form.

4.

MATCH UP
the questions to their answers.

BELIEVE IN GHOSTS? HOW OLD IS OFFICIALLY "GROWN UP"? IF YOU COULL

LD YOU WEAR A TUTU TO SCHOOL? WI

WATCH SPORTS OR PLAY SPORTS? DO YOU WANT TO GO SKYDIVING S

RAOKE SONG? DESCRIBE YOUR MOST EMBARRASSING BABY

EVER BEEN IN LOVE? WHAT'S YOUR MOST

THER BE NAMED IMA HOGG OR ANITA BATH? DID YOU USED

ERRIFIC OR TERRIFYING? WHICH SPORTS TEAM DO YOU HATE THE MOST?

FED ANIMAL? SMOOTH OR CHUNKY? DOES

CALLED "SWEETIE"? IS EVERYTHING BETTER WITH HOT SAUCE? IS SNC

RTOON CHARACTER AS A KID? HAVE YOU EVER WALKED

URP ON DEMAND? WHO SHOULD PLAY YOU

MOST? WHAT WORD DO YOU USE WAY, WAY TOO

SCHOOL SUBJECT (BESIDES LUNCH)? WOULD YOU RATHER READ MINDS

EAL FUR? DO YOU SING IN THE SHOWER?

OU DRESS UP YOUR DOG? EVER BROKEN ANY BONES? WHEN, WHERE, HOW?

BOUT YOURSELF? IF YOU COULD PICK YOUR OWN NICKNAME

REALLY? CLOWNS: TERRIFIC OR TERRIFY

BOUGHT A GIFT FOR AN ANIMAL? WOULD YOU EVER USE

RTUNE WOULD YOU LIKE TO FIND IN YOUR NEXT COOKIE? DO YOU SLEEP WITH

TOPS: TACKY OR TASTEFUL? WHAT ARE

METHING GROSS TO BE ON TV? DID YOU USED TO THINK YOUR TOYS CAME

OR BLACK LICORICE? WHAT IS THE WEIRDEST THING

SKIING? WHAT'S THE NASTIEST THING

YOU LIFT ONE EYEBROW? WILL YOU HAVE THE SAME B

GONE SKINNY-DIPPING? HOW EMBARRASSING ARE YOUR PARENTS? DC

DESCRIBE YOUR LOVE LIFE IN ONE WO

WHAT WOULD IT BE? WHAT ARE YOU HUNGRY FOR RIGHT NOW? DESCRIBE
RIGHT NOW? WOULD YOU RATHER BE NA
ME BEST FRIEND 10 YEARS FROM NOW? HOW HONEST ARE YOU, REALLY
ING WALKS IN GRAVEYARDS? WHAT'S THE NASTIEST
VE YOU EVER GONE SKINNY-DIPPING?
IS CAME ALIVE AT NIGHT? DO YOU OWN ANY TIE-DYED
TO SCHOOL WITH NO CLOTHES ON? HAVE YOU EVER BOUGHT A GIFT FOR
SOUND SMART? RED LICORICE OR BLACK
WHAT FORTUNE WOULD YOU LIKE TO FIND IN YOUR NEXT COOKIE?
GLASS DOOR? WHAT IS THE WEIRDEST THING IN YOUR BAG R
MOVIE OF YOUR LIFE? WHAT DO YOU LIKE
PARENTS PICK YOUR CLOTHES? WHAT'S YOUR FAVORITE S
PERMANENTLY PERFECT HAIR? DID YOU USED TO THINK YOUR TOYS CA
ANIMAL? CAN YOU LIFT ONE EYEBROW?
SPORTS OR PLAY SPORTS? EVER DREAMED YOU WENT TO SCHOOL WITH N
YOU WANT TO GO SKYDIVING SOMEDAY? WHAT D
LAST THING YOU ATE? DO YOU BELIEVE IN
RUSH? HAVE YOU EVER WALKED INTO A PLATE-GLASS DOOR?
RATHER GO TO A SINGLE-SEX OR CO-ED SCHOOL? DO YOU LIKE BEING CALLED
IGHT NOW? WOULD YOU WEAR REAL FUR
MOST EMBARRASSING BABY PICTURE. IS SNOWBOARDING COOLER THAN
HICH SPORTS TEAM DO YOU HATE THE MOST?
HAVE YOU EVER BEEN IN LOVE? DO YOU LIKE
OM NOW? WHO WAS YOUR FAVORITE CARTOON CHARACTER
GRAVEYARDS? WHAT'S YOUR FAVORITE SCHOOL SUBJECT (BESIDES
PARENTS NAG YOU ABOUT THE MOST? HAVE

Designer/Art Wrangler
Kayt de Fever

Art Director
Jill Turney

Editorial Contributor
Erin Conley

Production Editor
Jen Mills

Queen of All She Surveys
Patty Morris

Illustrators

Helen Dardik
Embarrassing Moments, Music,
Lying-Secrets-Gossip, Yikes

Jane Dixon
Names, Cats-Dogs-Critters,
Family, School

Jessie Hartland
Food, Style, Vacations-Travel,
Randomosity

Steve Kongsle
instructional art

Doreen Mulryan Marts
Love-Crushes, When I Was Little,
Friendship, Party

Luisa Montalto
introduction

Sean Sims
My Fortune, Sports,
Real Time, Books-Movies-TV

Thanks

David Avidor
Laurie Bryan

MORE GREAT BOOKS FROM KLUTZ

Bead Loom Bracelets

Friendship Bracelets

It's All About Me:
Personality Quizzes for
You & Your Friends

Just Between Friends

Me & My Friends:
The Book of Us

My All-Time Top 5:
A Book of Lists for
You and Your Friends

My Life According
to Me®

Paper-craft Cards:
Flowers

Room Lanterns

Shrink Art Jewelry

CAN'T GET ENOUGH?

Here are some simple ways to keep the Klutz coming.

Order more
of the supplies that
came with this book
at klutz.com.
It's quick, it's easy
and, seriously, where
else are you going to
find this exact stuff?

Get your hands
on a copy of
The Klutz Catalog.
To request a free
copy of our mail
order catalog, go to
klutz.com/catalog.

Become a Klutz Insider
and get e-mail about
new releases, special
offers, contests, games,
goofiness, and who-
knows-what-all. If you're
a grown-up who wants to
receive e-mail from Klutz,
head to klutz.com/insider.

If any of this sounds good to you, but you don't feel like going online right
now, just give us a call at 1-800-737-4123. We'd love to hear from you.